KINGDOM LIFE

FELLOWSHIP

CENTER INC.

THE SALVATION
BOOKLET

PASTOR EVA GRIER

PASTOR OF EDUCATION

BISHOP ERROL BECKLES, PH.D.

SENIOR PASTOR

1

TABLE OF CONTENTS

BISHOP ERROL BECKLES, PH.D.

IS THE FOUNDER, SENIOR PASTOR AND PRESIDENT OF KINGDOM LIFE FELLOWSHIP CENTER, INC. (K.L.F.C.)

CALLED BY GOD AT THE AGE OF TWELVE TO TAKE THE COMPLEX THINGS OF THE SCRIPTURE AND MAKE THEM SIMPLE, DR.

3

BECKLES HAS SPENT HIS LIFE STUDYING AND TEACHING THE BIBLE.

PRIOR TO FOUNDING K.L.F.C., HE PASTORED RESTORATION TEMPLE AND RESTORATION FULL GOSPEL TABERNACLE CHURCHES.

DR. BECKLES IS MARRIED TO LADY BEV, THE EXECUTIVE PASTOR AND FIRST LADY OF K. L. F. C.

PREFACE

I TRUST THAT THIS
BOOKLET WILL GIVE YOU
THE FOUNDATIONAL
PRINCIPLES OF
SALVATION. SALVATION
IS THE MOST IMPORTANT
SUBJECT MATTER IN THE
LIFE OF A PERSON. IT IS
THE ACT OF SAVING A
LIFE FROM DEATH ALONG
WITH DELIVERANCE
FROM THE PENALTY AND
POWER OF SIN. THOUGH,
IN ORDER TO TRULY

UNDERSTAND BIBLICAL SALVATION, YOU MUST COMPREHEND THE FOLLOWING: WHAT IS BIBLICAL SALVATION? WHY DO A PERSON NEED SALVATION? AND, HOW DO YOU OBTAIN SALVATION? I PRAY THAT THIS BOOKLET PROVIDES YOU WITH A CLEAR BIBLICAL UNDERSTANDING OF GOD'S FREE AND AWESOME GIFT OF SALVATION, WHICH WILL FOREVER CHANGE YOUR LIFE.

KINGDOM LIFE
FELLOWSHIP CENTER

IS THE BEGINNING OF THE FULFILLMENT OF A VISION THAT GOD GAVE TO ME ON THE MORNING OF JANUARY 3, 2000 AT 4:30 A.M. IN WHICH I WAS INSTRUCTED TO TAKE THE "CHURCH" INTO THE "KINGDOM OF GOD." I HAD NO IDEA AS TO WHAT THAT MEANT.

ALL I KNEW WAS

"CHURCH" (HAVING BEEN IN CHURCH SINCE I WAS TWO YEARS OLD), NEVERTHELESS I DECIDED TO STUDY THE SUBJECT OF THE CHURCH AND THE KINGDOM. WHAT I DISCOVERED CHANGED MY LIFE FOREVER... I WANTED ALL MY PASTOR FRIENDS TO GET THE REVELATION. I WANTED ALL THE MEMBERS OF THE CHURCH I WAS PASTORING TO EXPERIENCE WHAT I WAS FEELING BECAUSE I WAS

SURE THEY WOULD BE AS EXCITED AS I WAS. I WAS WRONG! NOBODY WAS INTERESTED... THE "CHURCH IS FINE," THEY ALL TOLD ME "DON'T START MESSING WITH A SYSTEM THAT HAS WORKED FOR HUNDREDS OF YEARS," MY CLOSEST FRIEND SAID TO ME. I UNSUCCESSFULLY TRIED TO EXPLAIN THAT THE "CHURCH" SYSTEM MUST BE REPLACED WITH THE SYSTEM OF THE KINGDOM. FOR TEN YEARS NO ONE WOULD

LISTEN, HOWEVER IT WAS WORKING FOR ME. FOR THE FIRST TIME IN MY LIFE I WAS EXPERIENCING THE FREEDOM AND ABUNDANT LIFE THAT JESUS PROMISED US. THEN, JUST OVER A YEAR AGO GOD BEGAN CONNECTING ME WITH THE CORE GROUP OF PEOPLE WHO ARE ASSIGNED TO BE THE PROTOTYPE OF WHAT KINGDOM LIVING IS ALL ABOUT. NOW, ALONG WITH MY WONDERFUL WIFE, LADY BEV, THE

FOUNDING LEADERS AND PARTNERS OF KINGDOM LIFE FELLOWSHIP CENTER, I AM READY TO BEGIN THE TASK OF CHANGING THE SYSTEM OF THE "CHURCH" INTO THE VISION, MISSION AND MANDATE OF THE KINGDOM OF GOD. IF YOU ARE TIRED OF DOING THE SAME THING YEAR AFTER YEAR WITH NO RESULTS, I INVITE YOU TO LEARN MORE ABOUT US AND THIS "GOD MOVEMENT."

INTRODUCTION

Salvation:

There is no subject that we can study that is more important than salvation. However, in order to help us better understand the subject of salvation, we must answer three important questions

What is Biblical Salvation?

Why do we need Salvation?

How do we obtain Salvation?

The Pew Polling Group conducted a study in 2009 and found that 83% of Americans claimed to be saved. However, when they were asked the follow up question what is salvation? More than 60% of them could not explain it.

There answers ranged from baptism to church membership.

It is therefore the intent of this hand book to ensure that you would know what biblical salvation really is for yourself, and that you would be able to explain it to others.

Question One

What is biblical salvation?

In order to understand salvation we must understand what it is.

The dictionary defines SALVATION as the act of snatching others by force from serious peril. In its most basic sense, salvation is the saving of a life from death or harm. Scripture, particularly the New Testament, extends salvation to include deliverance from the penalty and power of sin.

In the Old Testament salvation for the Israelite never carried a purely secular sense of deliverance from death or harm. Since God is the only source of biblical salvation, any saving act—even when the focus is preservation of life or release from national oppression—is a spiritual event.

The primary event of salvation in the Old Testament is the Exodus (Ex. 14:13) [And Moses said unto the people, Fear ye not, stand still, and see the salvation of the LORD, which he will show to you today: for the Egyptians whom ye have seen today, ye shall see them again no more forever.]

This act of salvation demonstrated both God's power to save and God's concern for His oppressed people (Ex. 34:6-7) [6And the LORD passed by before him, and proclaimed, The LORD, The LORD God, merciful and gracious, longsuffering, and abundant in goodness and truth, [7]Keeping mercy for thousands, forgiving iniquity and transgression and sin, and that will by no means clear *the guilty*; visiting the iniquity of the fathers upon the children, and upon the children's children, unto the third and to the fourth *generation*.]

Israel recounted God's deliverance or salvation

from Egyptian slavery in
three ways

1. The Passover ritual
(Ex. 12:1-13)

[¹And the LORD spake unto
Moses and Aaron in the
land of Egypt, saying, ²This
month *shall be* unto you the
beginning of months: it
shall be the first month of
the year to you. ³Speak ye
unto all the congregation of
Israel, saying, In the tenth
day of this month they shall
take to them every man a
lamb, according to the
house of *their* fathers, a
lamb for an house: ⁴And if

the household be too little
for the lamb, let him and his
neighbour next unto his
house take *it* according to
the number of the souls;
every man according to his
eating shall make your
count for the lamb. [5]Your
lamb shall be without
blemish, a male of the first
year: ye shall take *it* out
from the sheep, or from the
goats: [6]And ye shall keep it
up until the fourteenth day
of the same month: and the
whole assembly of the
congregation of Israel shall
kill it in the evening. [7]And
they shall take of the blood,
and strike *it* on the two side

posts and on the upper door post of the houses, wherein they shall eat it. ⁸And they shall eat the flesh in that night, roast with fire, and unleavened bread; *and* with bitter *herbs* they shall eat it. ⁹Eat not of it raw, nor sodden at all with water, but roast *with* fire; his head with his legs, and with the purtenance thereof. ¹⁰And ye shall let nothing of it remain until the morning; and that which remaineth of it until the morning ye shall burn with fire. ¹¹And thus shall ye eat it; *with* your loins girded, your shoes on your feet, and your staff in your hand; and ye shall eat it in haste: it *is* the LORD'S passover. ¹²For I will pass through the land of Egypt this night, and will smite all the firstborn in the land of Egypt, both man and beast; and against all the gods of Egypt I will execute judgment: I *am* the LORD. ¹³And the blood shall be to you for a token upon the houses where ye *are*: and when I see the blood, I will pass over you, and the plague shall not be upon you to destroy *you*, when I smite the land of Egypt.]

2. In sermon (Neh. 9:9-11)

[9And didst see the affliction of our fathers in Egypt, and heardest their cry by the Red sea; 10And showedst signs and wonders upon Pharaoh, and on all his servants, and on all the people of his land: for thou knewest that they dealt proudly against them. So didst thou get thee a name, as *it is* this day. 11And thou didst divide the sea before them, so that they went through the midst of the sea on the dry land; and their persecutors thou threwest into the deeps, as

a stone into the mighty
waters.]

3. In psalms (Psa.
74:12-13)

[For God *is* my King of old,
working salvation in
the midst of the
earth.]
13 [Thou didst divide the
sea by thy strength:
thou brakest the
heads of the dragons
in the waters.]

Salvation as defined in the
New Testament is the
deliverance of man not

from physical bondage but from the bondage of sin. The angel instructed Joseph to call Mary's baby Jesus because he will save his people from their sin

Matt 1:20-21

[20But while he thought on these things, behold, the angel of the Lord appeared unto him in a dream, saying, Joseph, thou son of David, fear not to take unto thee Mary thy wife: for that which is conceived in her is of the Holy Ghost. 21And she shall bring forth a son, and thou shalt call his name JESUS: for he shall save his people from their sins.]

This brings us to the second question

Question Two

Why do we need Salvation?

There are three main reasons why every human needs salvation

Reason One:

All men are in the bondage of sin.

We will deal with sin in another handbook however the bible makes it clear that all men are sinners.

We are sinners in two ways

1. By birth: we were all born in sin. Psa 51:5

[Behold, I was shapen in iniquity; and in sin did my mother conceive me.]

2.   By Choice: we
        have all chosen
        to commit sin.
        Rom 3:23

[For all have sinned, and
come short of the glory of
God;]

Reason Two:

The payment for our sin is
death.

   Romans 6:23

[For the wages of sin *is*
death; but the gift of God *is*

eternal life through Jesus Christ our Lord.]

In order to understand this we must go back to the first man and the first sin. In Genesis 2:17-18 after God had made man he command him not to eat of the tree of knowledge of good and evil

[But of the tree of the knowledge of good and evil, thou shalt not eat of it: for in the day that thou eatest thereof thou shalt surely die.]

In Genesis 3 man committed the first sin by disobeying God command and eating of the tree. The result of his actions was that all of his offspring suffer the same payment for their sin.

We read this fact in Romans 5:12

[12Wherefore, as by one man sin entered into the world, and death by sin; and so death passed upon all men, for that all have sinned:]

So now we know the bible teaches us that all men are sinners and all sinners are paid with death.

This brings us to the third reason why we all need salvation

Reason Three:

Jesus died for all of our sins so that all of us can live.

In Romans 5:8 and John 3:16-17 we read this fact.

[8But God commendeth his love toward us, in that,

while we were yet sinners,
Christ died for us.]

[16For God so loved the
world, that he gave his only
begotten Son, that
whosoever believeth in him
should not perish, but have
everlasting life. 17For God
sent not his Son into the
world to condemn the
world; but that the world
through him might be
saved.]

This bring us to our third
and final question

Question Three

How do I obtain salvation?

It is clear that I am a sinner, you are a sinner, we all are sinners by birth and by choice. It is also clear that our sin will lead us to the punishment of God. The good news however is the fact that God wants to save us rather than punish us.

The only step remaining therefore is our accepting or rejecting his gift of salvation.

To obtain salvation or to receive the gift that God is offering you is as easy as A.B.C.

A. – Acknowledge that you are a sinner.

B. – Believe that Jesus died for your sins

C. – Confess with your mouth that God has forgiven you.

It is just that simple my dear friend, it is just that

simple! You can't earn it, you can't buy it, you don't have to work for it. All you have to do is just believe it and receive it as God's gift for you.

In Romans 10:9 -10 we read

[That if thou shalt confess with thy mouth the Lord Jesus, and shalt believe in thine heart that God hath raised him from the dead, thou shalt be saved. [10]For with the heart man believeth unto righteousness; and with the mouth confession is made unto salvation.]

In Eph. 2:8- 9 we read

[For by grace are ye saved through faith; and that not of yourselves: *it is* the gift of God: [9]Not of works, lest any man should boast.]

Salvation is God's pardon to all mankind for all their sin

Let me encourage you to accept your pardon and live forever with God.

Your Turn

What are you going to do?

Now that you know God loves you so much that he sent his son to die for you, the only question left is what are you going to do.

Jesus has already done his part, he died for you. We have now done our part by telling you how easy it is for you to receive everlasting life.

Now it is all up to you!

You can decide to accept
your pardon from Jesus and
live forever with him, or
you can decide to reject him
and die without him.

If you decide to accept him
today, on the Day of
Judgment when all men
shall stand before him to be
judged, when your turn
comes to be judged he will
accept you and you will
hear him say well done
come live with me forever.

On the other hand if you
decide to reject him today,

on the Day of Judgment he will reject you and you will hear him say depart from me I never knew you.

My dear friend if you would like to accept Jesus today just says this simple prayer and mean it from your heart and you will receive salvation.

Dear God, I come to you a sinner in need of your salvation. I confess that I have done many wrong things but I ask you to forgive me of all of my sins,

wash me in the blood of
your son Jesus Christ and
make me your child. I
accept my pardon today
and ask for your help to live
to please for this day
forward in Jesus name I
pray Amen.

Congratulations! my friend
you are now saved.
Welcome to the body of
Christ and the start of your
brand new life.

Next Step

Now that you are saved there are a few important things that you need to do next.

First:

You must tell somebody about your salvation.

I recommend that you start by telling us at Kingdom Life Fellowship Center. As soon as you do we will help you with the next two important things you will need to do.

Feel free to call the fellowship at (302)858-0370 or email us at theklfc@gmail.com and someone from our Education or Outreach department will contact you.

Second:

You must begin to pray to God

I know that you may not know how to pray, however when you call or email us we will be more than happy to help you.

Third:

You must begin to read
your Bible

I recommend that you start
by reading the Gospel of
John it will help you in your
walk with God.

Fourth:

You must begin to fellowship
with other believers.

If you live in or near the state
of Delaware let me
personally invite you to be
my special guest this or any

Sunday at Kingdom Life
Fellowship Center.

When you visit I promise that
we will make you feel at
home from your very first
day.

So once again welcome to the
family of God… and I am
looking forward to seeing
you real soon.